HOME MADE FOOD NOTE BOOK

BIS Publishers
Building Het Sieraad
Postjesweg 1
1057 DT Amsterdam
The Netherlands
T +31 (0)20 515 02 30
F +31 (0)20 515 02 39
bis@bispublishers.com
www.bispublishers.com

ISBN 978 90 6369 397 8

Text, design & illustrations: Yvette van Boven

Copyright © 2015 Yvette van Boven and BIS Publishers.

Published in collaboration with Fontaine Publishers.

THIS BOOK BELONGS TO:

_____

TEL: _____

EMAIL: _____

IF YOU FIND
THIS BOOK
BECAUSE I
LOST IT, I WILL
PREPARE THE
DISH ON PAGE

AS A FINDER'S
FEE!

TABLE OF CONTENTS

HANDY STUFF

SHELF LIFE

STORE THESE
FRUITS
IN THE FRIDGE:

APPLES
APRICOTS
CANTALOUPE
FIGS
HONEYDEW
MELON

STORE THIS AT
ROOM TEMPERATURE:

AVOCADO'S
UNRIPE BANANAS
NECTARINES
PEACHES
PEARS
PLUM & TOMATOES

ALSO STORE THESE FRUIT & VEG IN THE FRIDGE,
BUT KEEP SEPERATE FROM THE FOODS LISTED
ABOVE. (THE ETHYLENE GAS THAT IS RELEASED
WILL CAUSE THESE FRUITS TO SPOIL FASTER.

RIPE BANANAS, CAULIFLOWER, LETTUCE (ALL VARIETIES)
POTATOES, SWEET POTATOES, BROCCOLI, ALL CABBAGE OR
KALE VARIETIES, CUCUMBER, AUBERGINE, GREEN
PEAS & BEANS, PARSLEY & OTHER HERBS, PEPPERS,
PUMPKIN, WATERMELON AND CARROTS.

STORE IN THE FRIDGE FOR HOW LONG?

1-3 DAYS

STRAWBERRIES
ARTICHOKES
ASPARAGUS
BANANAS (RIPE)
BASIL
BROCCOLI
MUSHROOMS
DILL
MIZUNA (AND OTHER
VARIETIES OF LOOSE
LEAF LETTUCE)
CORN
CHERRIES
FRENCH BEANS
WATERCRESS

LONGER

POTATOES
APPLES
BEETROOT
CABBAGE
PUMPKIN
CELERY
CELERIAC
CARROTS

4-5 DAYS

PINEAPPLE
AUBERGINE
COURGETTE
GRAPES
CANTALOUPE
CUCUMBER
HONEYDEW MELON
LIME
ROCKET
LETTUCE

5-7 DAYS

WATERMELON
TOMATOES
BRUSSELS SPROUTS
SPINACH
ORANGES
PLUMS
LEEKS
PARSLEY
PEPPER
OREGANO
MINT
GRAPEFRUIT
LEMONS
BLUEBERRIES
CAULIFLOWER
APRICOTS

STORAGE TiPS

PRODUCT	FRiDGE after opening	cupBoARD unopened
Pickles	3 months	1 year
Vinegar	unnecessary	open: 1 year
		unopened: 2 years
Baking powder	never	6 months
Beer	1 day	9 months
Flour	never	1 year
Beans (dry)	never	2 year
Butter	2 weeks	never
Bread	never	2-4 days
Couscous	never	1 year
Dried fruit	never	open: 1 month
		unopened: 6 months
Honey	6 months	1 year
Jam & jelly	6 months	1 year
Ketchup	6 months	1 year
Biscuits (packed)	never	open: 1 month
		unopened: 2 months
Homemade Mayo	3 days	never
Cornflour	never	1 year
Mustard	unnecessary	1 year
Nuts	unnecessary	open: 3 months
		unopened: 6 month
Cooking Oils	unnecessary	open: upto 6 month
		unopened:
		6 months-1 year

PRODUCT	FRIDGE after opening	cupBoARD unopened
Olives /in oil	2-4 weeks	6 months
Olives /brined	2 weeks	$1\frac{1}{2}$ years
Breadcrumbs	never	6 months
Pasta: FRESH	2 days	never
Pasta: DRY	never	2 years
Pesto	3 days	6 months
Peanut butter	unnecessary	open: 6 months unopened: 1 year
Fizzy drinks	2 days	6 months
Rice: WHITE	never	open: 1 year unopened: 2 year
Rice: BROWN	never	open: 6 months unopened: 1 year
Juice (container)	10 days	6 months
Juice (Freshly squeezed)	3 days	never
Spices	never	ground: 2 year whole: 3 year
Wine (table-)	3 days	1 year
Worcestershire sauce	never	open: 1 year unopened: 1 year

UNITS OF VOLUME

 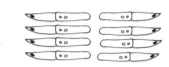 1 teaspoon = 5 ml = 8 pinches

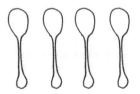 3 teaspoons = 15 ml = 1 tablespoon

2 tablespoons = 30 ml = 1 fluid ounce

4 tablespoons = 60 ml = 2 fluid ounces = $\frac{1}{4}$ cup

 4 fluid ounces = 120 ml = $\frac{1}{2}$ cup

 8 fluid ounces = 240 ml = 1 cup

2 cups = 480 ml = 1 pint (475 ml)

 4 cups = 960 ml = 2 pints = 1 quart (950 ml)

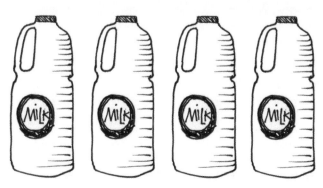 4 quarts = 4500 ml = 1 gallon

WEIGHT

1 ounce(1 OZ) = 28,5 grams

1 pound (1 LBS) = 454 grams

2 pounds (2 LBS) = 908 grams (almost 1 kilo)

1 Ton = 1000 kilograms

OVEN TEMPERATURE

GAS	°C		°F	
1	140		275	low
2	150		300	low
3	165		325	medium
4	175		350	medium
5	190		375	medium-high
6	200		400	medium-high
7	220		425	hot
8	230		450	hot
9	240		475	very high
10	260		500	very high

FiSH, POiSSON, FiSCH,PESCADO

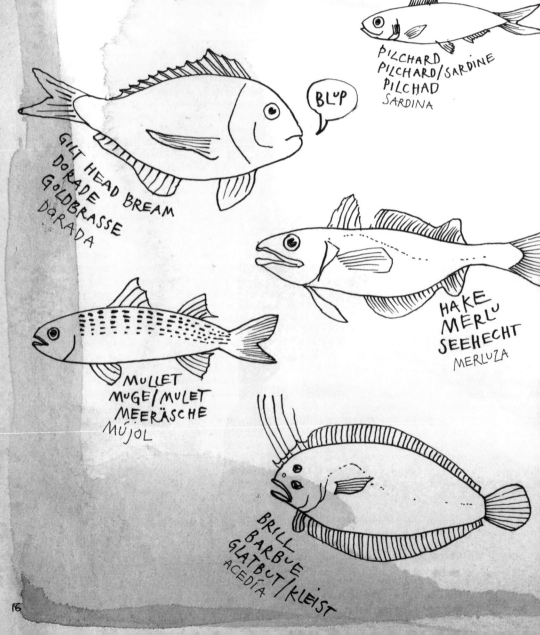

BLUP

PILCHARD
PILCHARD/SARDINE
PILCHAD
SARDINA

GILT HEAD BREAM
DORADE
GOLDBRASSE
DORADA

HAKE
MERLU
SEEHECHT
MERLUZA

MULLET
MUGE/MULET
MEERÄSCHE
MÚJOL

BRILL
BARBUE
GLATBUT/KLEIST
ACEDÍA

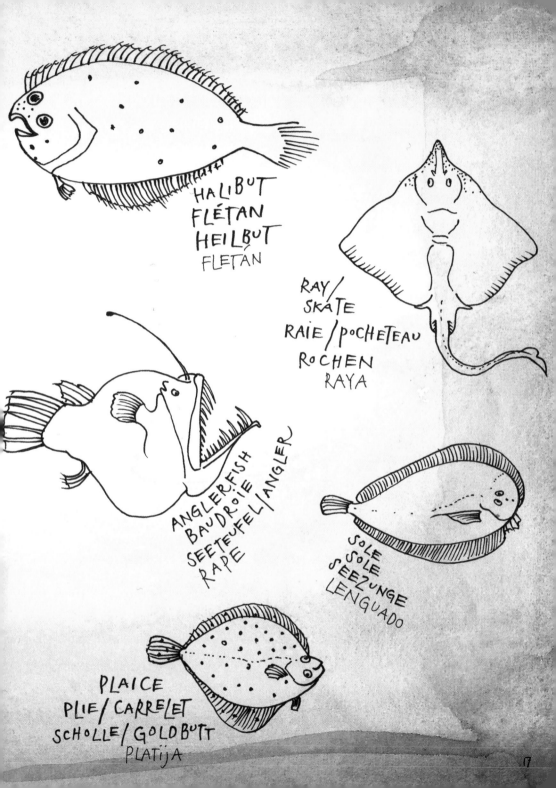

HALIBUT
FLÉTAN
HEILBUT
FLETÁN

RAY/
SKATE
RAIE/POCHETEAU
ROCHEN
RAYA

ANGLERFISH
BAUDROIE
SEETEUFEL/ANGLER
RAPE

SOLE
SOLE
SEEZUNGE
LENGUADO

PLAICE
PLIE/CARRELET
SCHOLLE/GOLDBUTT
PLATIJA

COD
CABILLAUD/MORUE
KABELJAU/DORSCH
BACALAO

GOATFISH
ROUGET
MEER BARBE
SALMONETE

JOHN DORY
SAINT PIERRE
PETERSFISCH
PEZ DE SAN PEDRO

18

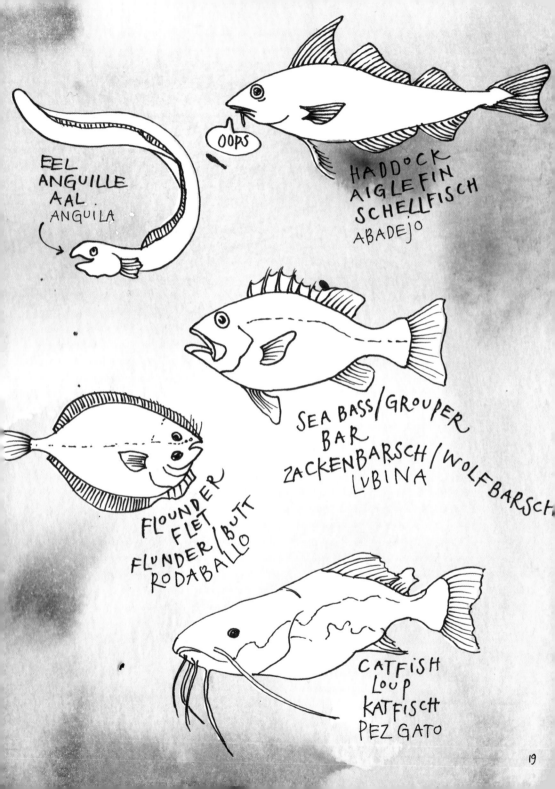

EEL
ANGUILLE
AAL.
ANGUILA

OOPS

HADDOCK
AIGLEFIN
SCHELLFISCH
ABADEJO

SEA BASS/GROUPER
BAR
ZACKENBARSCH/WOLFBARSCH
LUBINA

FLOUNDER
FLET
FLUNDER/BUTT
RODABALLO

CATFISH
LOUP
KATFISCH
PEZ GATO

19

SHELLFISH & CRUSTACEANS, COQUILLAGES & CRUSTACES KRUSTEN- & SCHALENTIERE MOLUSCO & MARISCO

RAZOR SHELL
COUTEAU.
MEERSCHEIDE
NAVAJA

MUSSEL
MOULE
MIESMUSCHEL
MEJILLON

CRAB
CRABE
KURZSCHWANZKREBS
CANGREJO

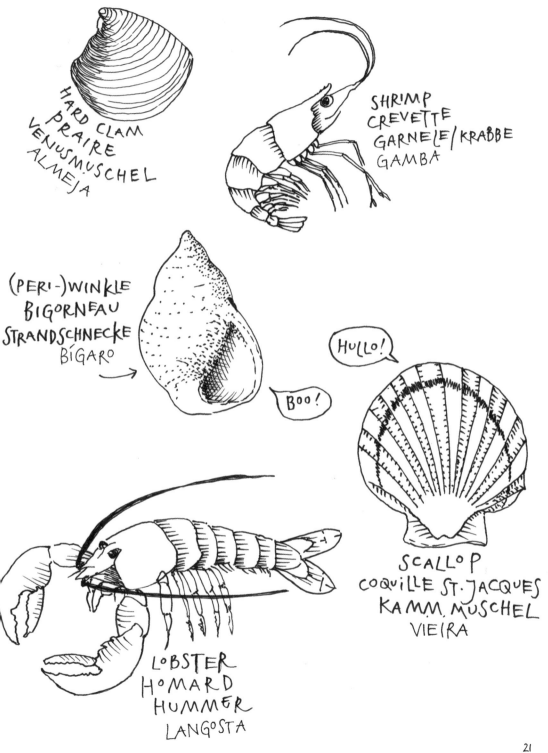

VEGETABLES, VEGETABLES, GEMÜSE, VERDURAS

CUCUMBER
CONCOMBRE
GURKE
PEPINO

GARLIC
AIL
KNOBLAUCH
AJO

CARROT
CAROTTE
KAROTTE
ZANAHORIA

BROAD BEANS (FAVA BEANS)
FÈVES
SAUBOHNEN
HABAS

BEETROOT
BETTERAVE
ROTE BETE
REMOLACHA

ONION
OIGNON
ZWIEBEL
CEBOLLA

BELL PEPPER
POIVRON
PAPRIKASCHOTE
PAPRIKA

FENNEL
FENOUIL
FENCHEL
HINOJO

CURLY KALE
CHOU FRISÉ
GRÜNKOHL
COL RIZADA

ZUCCHINI
COURGETTE
ZUCCHINI
CALABACÍN

RADISH
RADIS
RETTICH
RÁBANO

SPINACH
ÉPINARDS
SPINAT
ESPINACAS

ARUGULA
ROQUETTE
RUCOLA
RÚCULA

MUSHROOM
CHAMPIGNON
PILZ
CHAMPIÑÓN

EGGPLANT
AUBERGINE
AUBERGINE
BERENJENA

LEEK
POIREAU
LAUCH
PUERRO

CAULIFLOWER
CHOUFLEUR
BLUMENKOHL
COLIFLOR

GREEN BEANS
GRÜNE BOHNEN
HARICOTS VERTS
JUDÍAS VERDES

HARICOTS VERTS
HARICOTS VERTS
GRÜNE BOHNEN
HABICHUELAS VERDES

23

MY
KITCHEN

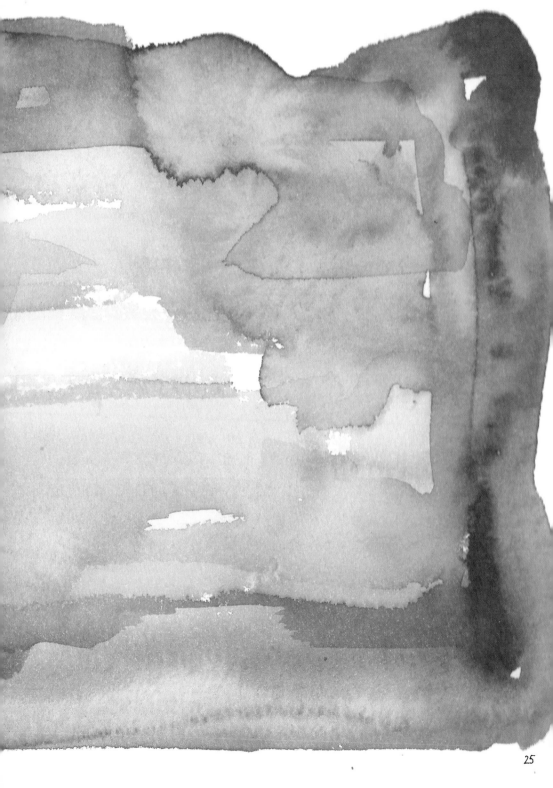

MY PANTRY

GRAINS RICE & PASTA

Spaghetti
{including whole
wheat!}
Penne
{other pasta va-
rieties, shells,
lagasne sheets,
pipe rigate and the
like}
Risotto rice
{preferably
Arborio rice}
Brown rice
Basmati rice
Wild Rice
{for a salad}
Bulgur
Couscous
Freekeh
Spelt or Farro
Pearl Barley
Quinoa
Polenta
Cornflour
Breadcrumbs
{preferably home-
made or panko}

BAKING INGREDIENTS

Flour
Wholemeal flour
Almond flour
Spelt flour
Rye flour
Maize flour
Baking powder
Baking soda
Instant yeast
Cacoa
Honey
Maple syrup
Golden syrup
Agave syrup
Sugar
Soft sugar
{dark brown, light
brown and white}
Icing sugar
Vanilla-extract
Raisins
Currants
Dried fruit

SPICE RACK

Seasalt
Maldon zout
Black pepper
{and pink and
white!}
Thyme
Oregano
Rosemary
Ground paprika
{sweet, hot and
smoked}
Curry powder
Cayenne
Chilli peppers
Cinnamon
Nutmeg
Ground Ginger
Allspice
Coriander seeds
Cumin
Caraway
Cardamom
Star aniseeds
Fennel seeds
Mustard seeds
Chinese
5-spice powder

LEGUMES NUTS & SEEDS

Hazelnuts
Walnuts
Almonds
Sunflower-&
pumpkin seeds
Linseeds
Canellini beans
Borlotti beans
Chickpeas
Lentils
{red, Du Puy &
green}
Split peas
Sesame seeds
Poppy seeds

JARS & TINS

Canned tomatoes
Tomato purée
Tahini
Tuna
Salmon
Sardines
Anchovies
Pearl Onions
Cornichons
{tiny pickles}
Capers
Olives
Canellini beans
Borlotti beans
Chickpeas
Kidneybeans
Black beans
Horseradish
Artichoke
hearts

OIL, VINEGAR & SAUCES

Extra virgin
Olive oil
Sunflower oil
Nut oil
Coconut oil
Grape seed oil
White wine
vinegar
Red wine
vinegar
Balsamic vinegar
Apple cider
vinegar
Rice vinegar
Mustard
{fine and coarse}
Mayonnaise
Ketchup
Sriracha
Tabasco
{red and green for
oysters}
Fish sauce
Sambal
Soy sauce
Light soy sauce
{Kikkoman}
Worcestershire
sauce

KETCHUP

for about 4 jars
of 250 ml

2½ kg/5½ lb tomatoes
1 red capsicum/pepper
2 onions, finely chopped
1 clove of garlic, crushed
100 ml/½ cup vinegar
75 grams/⅓ cup sugar
pinch of salt
2 tsp grated ginger
2 tsp ground paprika
2 tsp nutmeg
pinch of cayenne pepper
1 tbsp coriander seed
1 clove
freshly ground black pepper

Wash and chop the
tomatoes. Wash and chop the
red pepper. Remove the seeds.

Combine the tomatoes, red
pepper, onions and garlic in
a pan. Add a dash of water
and allow the ingredients
to simmer for approximately
1 hour. Stir occasionally
to prevent the mixture from
burning. Add a little water if
necessary.

Remove the sauce from the heat
and purée until smooth with
a hand blender. Return the
sauce back to the heat and
stir in the vinegar, sugar and
remaining spices.

Leave the sauce to simmer for
a further 1½ hours or until it
has sufficiently reduced.

Season with salt and pepper to
tasts. Pour the hot sauce into
sterilized jars.

Seal the jars with a suitable
clean lid and turn upside down
until cooled.

Ketchup has a shelflife of
1 year. Once opened, the jar
needs to be kept refrigerated.

HOME MADE KET-CHUP

MUSTARD MAYO

Ensure that all ingredients are at room temperature.

Whisk the egg yolk, black pepper, salt, lemon juice and mustard together in a bowl.

While stirring with a mixer, blend the sunflower oil with the egg mixture. First, a little at a time, then pour in a steady stream into a thick, creamy mayonnaise.

OH! BE CAREFUL:

This mayonnaise should be kept cool and preferably eaten within a few days since it contains raw egg.

for 1 jar

1 egg yolk
2 tbsp lemon juice or vinegar
2 tbsp coarse mustard
(or fine if preferred)
about 200 ml/¾ cup sunflower oil or as much as needed
Freshly ground black pepper and salt

MUSTARD

for 1 jar

100 grams/4oz mustard seed
200 ml/¾ cup white wine vinegar
(or of choice)
pepper and salt

You can soak the mustard seeds in the vinegar overnight for a smoother effect, but it's not absolutely necessary.

Blitz the mustard seed, vinegar, pepper and salt in a food processor.
It takes about 6 minutes to produce a semi-smooth mustard. Blitz longer for a smoother result.

Spoon the mustard into a jar. Close the lid and place in the fridge until ready to use.
It will get better in time.

RASPBERRY VINEGAR

for ½ litre

1½ cups/250 g raspberries
2 cups/500 ml white wine
vinegar
⅓ cup/60 g superfine sugar

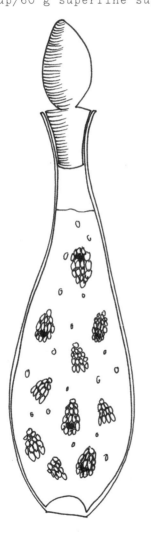

Put the raspberries in a bowl and pour in the vinegar. Cover and let stand at room temperature for 2 weeks.

Once in a while, press the raspberries against the side of the bowl with a spoon to release their juice.

Place a sieve over a saucepan and pour the raspberries and vinegar into it. Use a spoon to gently press down on the raspberries to drain the juice from them.

Be sure not to press down too hard or the vinegar will be cloudy.

Add the sugar to the vinegar and slowly bring the mixture to near boiling, stirring until the sugar has dissolved.

Pour the vinegar into spotlessly clean glass bottles and close them off with a cork or a lid. You can keep your home made vinegar in a cool dark room for over 6 months.

TIP!

Combining the vinegar with some nut oil and a drop of honey makes a delicious vinaigrette to drizzle over a goat cheese or chicken salad.

HERB-INFUSED OIL

for about 250 ml

2-3 sprigs of thyme, clean
2-3 sprigs of rosemary
2 dried chilli peppers
4 dried bay leaves
1 cup/250 ml light olive oil
a few black peppercorns

Preheat the oven to 125°F/50°C max. Put the thyme and rosemary on a baking sheet and bake until they are bone-dry, about 1 hour.

Put the herbs, peppers, bay leaves, and peppercorns in a jar, pour the oil on top, and let the mixture stand for at least 2 weeks before using.

LEMON VERBENA OIL

for about 250 ml

3 tbsp dried lemon verbena
1 cup/250 ml olive oil

Process the lemon verbena briefly in a food processor or mortar to break it up.

Add the oil and stir well. Pour the oil into a small saucepan and bring it to a boil.

Remove from the heat and pour through a sieve into a measuring cup with a spout. Don't stir or press the oil in the sieve or the oil will become cloudy—exercise some patience until it seeps through. Keep the oil in a very clean, dry bottle.

HOW TO MAKE BUTTER

for 1 bar about 250 grams/¾ cup
you will need:

1 litre/4,5 cups whipping cream
or heavy cream

Beat the cream for a long
time, with a mixer, until it
looks like scrambled eggs.

Pour the cream into
a clean dish towel that you've
placed over a strainer.
Collect the whey (the liquid)
in a bowl; you can use it to
make soda bread.

Wring the butter as much as
possible.

Knead it in a bowl of ice
water, changing the water 2
or 3 times, until the water
remains clear. This step is
important because if there's
any whey left, the butter can
quickly turn rancid.

Soak two wooden spatulas in
another bowl of cold water.
Use them to shape the butter
into a nice bar.

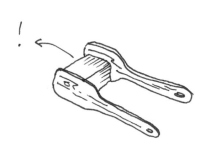

Wrap your butter in parchment
paper and store in the fridge.

It will remain fresh for at
least 2 weeks!

DRESSINGS!

SWEET & SOUR
CORIANDER
(CILANTRO)
DRESSING

BLEND TOGETHER:
1 BUNCH CORIANDER
   (CILANTRO)
½ RED ONION
1 TBSB HONEY
   (OR MORE)
1 TSP CURRY POWDER
1 RED PEPPER, SEEDS
            REMOVED
4 TBSP RED WINE VINEGAR
0,65 CUP / 150 ML OLIVE OIL

SMOKEY
MUSTARD
DRESSING

MIX:

2 TBSP MUSTARD
1 CLOVE OF GARLIC
1 TSP SMOKED
GROUND PAPRIKA
& 50 ML (2TBSP)
WHITE WINE
VINEGAR
WITH A HAND
BLENDER UNTIL
SMOOTH

WHISK 150 ML/
0,65 CUP GRAPE
SEED OIL INTO
THE MIXTURE
UNTIL BINDED

YOGURT
WALNUT
DRESSING

WHISK 1 TBSP
HONEY WITH
100 ML / 0.42 CUP
WHITE WINE
VINEGAR &
125 ML / ½ CUP
YOGHURT. STIR
IN 75 ML / ⅓ CUP
WALNUT OIL

SEASON
TO TASTE

33

YOUR KITCHEN

WINE NOTES

COLOUR (CIRCLE A GLASS)

WHITE   ROSÉ   RED   SPARKLING

COUNTRY : _____
REGION : _____
SUBREGION : _____
APPELLATION : _____
DOMAIN : _____
YEAR : _____
GRAPE : _____

WHEN :   : .. / .. / ....
WITH WHOM : _____
_____

WHAT WAS ON THE MENU ?
_____
_____

NOTES : _____

COLOUR (CIRCLE A GLASS)

WHITE   ROSÉ   RED   SPARKLING

COUNTRY : _____
REGION : _____
SUBREGION : _____
APPELLATION : _____
DOMAIN : _____
YEAR : _____
GRAPE : _____

WHEN :   : .. / .. / ....
WITH WHOM : _____
_____

WHAT WAS ON THE MENU ?
_____
_____

NOTES : _____

COLOUR (CIRCLE A GLASS)

WHITE   ROSÉ   RED   SPARKLING

COUNTRY : _____
REGION: _____
SUBREGION : _____
APPELLATION : _____
DOMAIN : _____
YEAR : _____
GRAPE : _____

WHEN :   : .. / .. / ....
WITH WHOM : _____
_____

WHAT WAS ON THE MENU ?
_____
_____

NOTES : _____
_____

COLOUR (CIRCLE A GLASS)

WHITE   ROSÉ   RED   SPARKLING

COUNTRY : _____
REGION: _____
SUBREGION : _____
APPELLATION : _____
DOMAIN : _____
YEAR : _____
GRAPE : _____

WHEN :   : .. / .. / ....
WITH WHOM : _____
_____

WHAT WAS ON THE MENU ?
_____
_____

NOTES : _____
_____

COLOUR (CIRCLE A GLASS)

WHITE   ROSÉ   RED   SPARKLING

COUNTRY : _____
REGION : _____
SUBREGION : _____
APPELLATION : _____
DOMAIN : _____
YEAR : _____
GRAPE : _____

WHEN :   : .. / .. / ....
WITH WHOM : _____
_____

WHAT WAS ON THE MENU ?
_____
_____

NOTES : _____
_____
_____

COLOUR (CIRCLE A GLASS)

WHITE   ROSÉ   RED   SPARKLING

COUNTRY : _____
REGION : _____
SUBREGION : _____
APPELLATION : _____
DOMAIN : _____
YEAR : _____
GRAPE : _____

WHEN :   : .. / .. / ....
WITH WHOM : _____
_____

WHAT WAS ON THE MENU ?
_____
_____

NOTES : _____
_____
_____

COLOUR (CIRCLE A GLASS)

WHITE   ROSÉ   RED   SPARKLING

COUNTRY : _____

REGION : _____

SUBREGION : _____

APPELLATION : _____

DOMAIN : _____

YEAR : _____

GRAPE : _____

WHEN : : .. / .. / ...

WITH WHOM : _____
_____

WHAT WAS ON THE MENU ?
_____
_____

NOTES : _____
_____

COLOUR (CIRCLE A GLASS)

WHITE   ROSÉ   RED   SPARKLING

COUNTRY : _____

REGION : _____

SUBREGION : _____

APPELLATION : _____

DOMAIN : _____

YEAR : _____

GRAPE : _____

WHEN : : .. / .. / ...

WITH WHOM : _____
_____

WHAT WAS ON THE MENU ?
_____
_____

NOTES : _____
_____

COLOUR (CIRCLE A GLASS)

WHITE   ROSÉ   RED   SPARKLING

COUNTRY : _____
REGION : _____
SUBREGION : _____
APPELLATION : _____
DOMAIN : _____
YEAR : _____
GRAPE : _____

WHEN :   : .. / .. / ....
WITH WHOM : _____
_____
_____

WHAT WAS ON THE MENU ?
_____
_____
_____

NOTES : _____
_____
_____

COLOUR (CIRCLE A GLASS)

WHITE   ROSÉ   RED   SPARKLING

COUNTRY : _____
REGION : _____
SUBREGION : _____
APPELLATION : _____
DOMAIN : _____
YEAR : _____
GRAPE : _____

WHEN :   : .. / .. / ....
WITH WHOM : _____
_____
_____

WHAT WAS ON THE MENU ?
_____
_____
_____

NOTES : _____
_____
_____

COLOUR (CIRCLE A GLASS)

WHITE   ROSÉ   RED   SPARKLING

COUNTRY : _____
REGION : _____
SUBREGION : _____
APPELLATION : _____
DOMAIN : _____
YEAR : _____
GRAPE : _____

WHEN :   : .. / .. / ....
WITH WHOM : _____
_____

WHAT WAS ON THE MENU ?
_____
_____
_____

NOTES : _____
_____

COLOUR (CIRCLE A GLASS)

WHITE   ROSÉ   RED   SPARKLING

COUNTRY : _____
REGION : _____
SUBREGION : _____
APPELLATION : _____
DOMAIN : _____
YEAR : _____
GRAPE : _____

WHEN :   : .. / .. / ....
WITH WHOM : _____
_____

WHAT WAS ON THE MENU ?
_____
_____
_____

NOTES : _____
_____

COLOUR (CIRCLE A GLASS)

WHITE   ROSÉ   RED   SPARKLING

COUNTRY : _____

REGION : _____

SUBREGION : _____

APPELLATION : _____

DOMAIN : _____

YEAR : _____

GRAPE : _____

WHEN :   : .. / .. / ....

WITH WHOM : _____

_____

WHAT WAS ON THE MENU ?

_____

_____

NOTES : _____

_____

_____

COLOUR (CIRCLE A GLASS)

WHITE   ROSÉ   RED   SPARKLING

COUNTRY : _____

REGION : _____

SUBREGION : _____

APPELLATION : _____

DOMAIN : _____

YEAR : _____

GRAPE : _____

WHEN :   : .. / .. / ....

WITH WHOM : _____

_____

WHAT WAS ON THE MENU ?

_____

_____

NOTES : _____

_____

_____

COLOUR (CIRCLE A GLASS)

WHITE   ROSÉ   RED   SPARKLING

COUNTRY : _____
REGION : _____
SUBREGION : _____
APPELLATION : _____
DOMAIN : _____
YEAR : _____
GRAPE : _____

WHEN : : .. / .. / ....
WITH WHOM : _____
_____

WHAT WAS ON THE MENU ?
_____
_____

NOTES : _____
_____
_____

COLOUR (CIRCLE A GLASS)

WHITE   ROSÉ   RED   SPARKLING

COUNTRY : _____
REGION : _____
SUBREGION : _____
APPELLATION : _____
DOMAIN : _____
YEAR : _____
GRAPE : _____

WHEN : : .. / .. / ....
WITH WHOM : _____
_____

WHAT WAS ON THE MENU ?
_____
_____

NOTES : _____
_____

43

COCKTAILS
(WELL, THE ONES YOU CAN STILL REMEMBER)

COCKTAIL NAME:

WHAT WAS IN IT:

WHEN DID YOU DRINK IT:

AND WITH WHOM:

COCKTAIL NAME:

WHAT WAS IN IT:

WHEN DID YOU DRINK IT:

AND WITH WHOM:

COCKTAIL NAME:

WHAT WAS IN IT:

WHEN DID YOU DRINK IT:

AND WITH WHOM:

COCKTAIL NAME:

WHAT WAS IN IT:

WHEN DID YOU DRINK IT:

AND WITH WHOM:

COCKTAIL NAME:

WHAT WAS IN IT:

WHEN DID YOU DRINK IT:

AND WITH WHOM:

COCKTAIL NAME:

WHAT WAS IN IT:

WHEN DID YOU DRINK IT:

AND WITH WHOM:

COCKTAIL NAME:

WHAT WAS IN IT:

WHEN DID YOU DRINK IT:

AND WITH WHOM:

COCKTAIL NAME:

WHAT WAS IN IT:

WHEN DID YOU DRINK IT:

AND WITH WHOM:

COCKTAIL NAME:

WHAT WAS IN IT:

WHEN DID YOU DRINK IT:

AND WITH WHOM:

COCKTAIL NAME:

WHAT WAS IN IT:

WHEN DID YOU DRINK IT:

AND WITH WHOM:

COCKTAIL NAME:

WHAT WAS IN IT:

WHEN DID YOU DRINK IT:

AND WITH WHOM:

COCKTAIL NAME:

WHAT WAS IN IT:

WHEN DID YOU DRINK IT:

AND WITH WHOM:

COCKTAIL NAME:

WHAT WAS IN IT:

WHEN DID YOU DRINK IT:

AND WITH WHOM:

COCKTAIL NAME:

WHAT WAS IN IT:

WHEN DID YOU DRINK IT:

AND WITH WHOM:

DRiNK MORE WATER!

a handy dandy checklist to get started

MONDAY

TUESDAY

WEDNESDAY

THURSDAY

FRIDAY

SATURDAY

SUNDAY

BLUB!!

ALLERGY & DiET LiST
DON'T POISON YOUR FAMiLY & FRIENDS!

NAME FRIEND: DOESN'T EAT:

ONLY
PALEO!

THANKS!

50

NAME FRIEND:

DOESN'T EAT:

UMM... HONEY, WHAT DID YOU PUT IN THE SOUP?

ZZZZ

RESTAURANT LIST
JOT DOWN THOSE GOOD TIPS BEFORE YOU FORGET THEM.

WHERE SHOULD
WE HAVE LUNCH
LATER ON?

MEMORABLE HOLIDAY EATS

LOOK UP THE RECIPES OF THIS LIST WHEN YOU'RE BACK HOME

(CHRISTMAS) PARTY PLANNER

EVENT/PARTY: DATE/TIME:

MENU: RECIPE SOURCE:

a week ahead:

on the day
itself:

2 days in advance:

1 day in advance:

(CHRISTMAS) PARTY PLANNER

EVENT/PARTY: DATE/TIME:

MENU: RECIPE SOURCE:

a week ahead: on the day itself:

2 days in advance:

1 day in advance:

(CHRISTMAS) PARTY PLANNER

EVENT/PARTY:

DATE/TIME:

MENU:

RECIPE SOURCE:

a week ahead: on the day itself:

2 days in advance:

1 day in advance:

JONGLE BIPS!

(CHRISTMAS) PARTY PLANNER

EVENT/PARTY: DATE/TIME:

MENU: RECIPE SOURCE:

_____   _____
_____   _____
_____   _____
_____   _____
_____   _____
_____   _____
_____   _____
_____   _____
_____   _____
_____   _____
_____   _____
_____   _____
_____   _____
_____   _____
_____   _____
_____   _____
_____   _____
_____   _____
_____   _____

a week ahead: on the day itself:

2 days in advance:

1 day in advance:

YOUR RECIPES

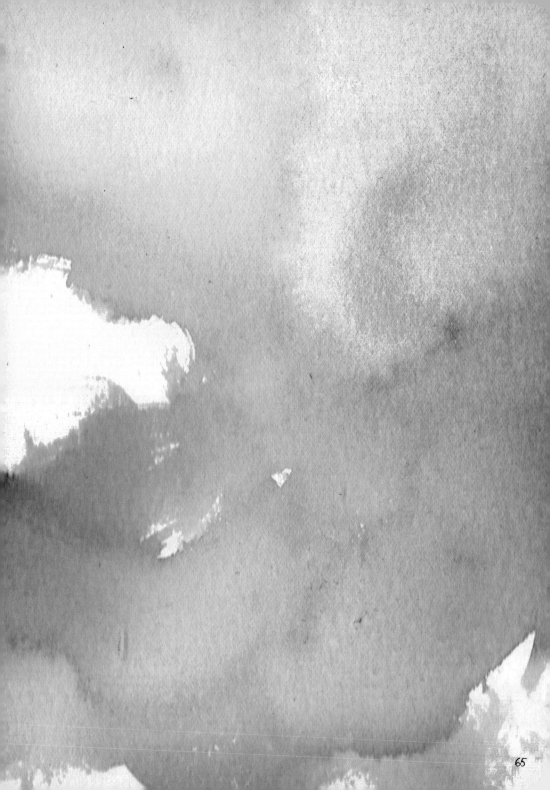

RECIPE FOR: _____

GIVEN TO ME BY: _____

DATE: _____

NUMBER OF SERVINGS: _____ RECIPE TYPE: _____

_____

_____

_____

_____

_____

_____

_____

_____

_____

_____

_____

_____

_____

_____

_____

_____

_____

_____

CHEERS!

RECIPE FOR:

GIVEN TO ME BY:

DATE:

NUMBER OF SERVINGS: RECIPE TYPE:

RECIPE FOR:

GIVEN TO ME BY:

DATE:

NUMBER OF SERVINGS: RECIPE TYPE:

RECIPE FOR:

GIVEN TO ME BY:

DATE:

NUMBER OF SERVINGS: RECIPE TYPE:

RECIPE FOR:

GIVEN TO ME BY:

DATE:

NUMBER OF SERVINGS: RECIPE TYPE:

RECIPE FOR:

GIVEN TO ME BY:

DATE:

NUMBER OF SERVINGS: RECIPE TYPE:

RECIPE FOR: _____

GIVEN TO ME BY: _____

DATE: _____

NUMBER OF SERVINGS: _____ RECIPE TYPE: _____

_____

_____

_____

_____

_____

_____

_____

_____

_____

_____

_____

_____

_____

_____

_____

_____

_____

_____

_____

_____

_____

RECIPE FOR:

GIVEN TO ME BY:

DATE:

NUMBER OF SERVINGS: RECIPE TYPE:

RECIPE FOR:

GIVEN TO ME BY:

DATE:

NUMBER OF SERVINGS: RECIPE TYPE:

RECIPE FOR: _____

GIVEN TO ME BY: _____

DATE: _____

NUMBER OF SERVINGS: _____ RECIPE TYPE: _____

RECIPE FOR:

GIVEN TO ME BY:

DATE:

NUMBER OF SERVINGS: RECIPE TYPE:

RECIPE FOR:

GIVEN TO ME BY:

DATE:

NUMBER OF SERVINGS: RECIPE TYPE:

RECIPE FOR:

GIVEN TO ME BY:

DATE:

NUMBER OF SERVINGS: RECIPE TYPE:

RECIPE FOR:

GIVEN TO ME BY:

DATE:

NUMBER OF SERVINGS: RECIPE TYPE:

RECIPE FOR:

GIVEN TO ME BY:

DATE:

NUMBER OF SERVINGS: RECIPE TYPE:

YEAH SURE...
CARROTS
ARE GOOD
FOR YOUR
EYE'S...
-SIGH-

RECIPE FOR:

GIVEN TO ME BY:

DATE:

NUMBER OF SERVINGS: RECIPE TYPE:

RECIPE FOR:

GIVEN TO ME BY:

DATE:

NUMBER OF SERVINGS: RECIPE TYPE:

RECIPE FOR:

GIVEN TO ME BY:

DATE:

NUMBER OF SERVINGS: RECIPE TYPE:

RECIPE FOR:

GIVEN TO ME BY:

DATE:

NUMBER OF SERVINGS: RECIPE TYPE:

HUNGRY!

RECIPE FOR:

GIVEN TO ME BY:

DATE:

NUMBER OF SERVINGS: RECIPE TYPE:

RECIPE FOR:

GIVEN TO ME BY:

DATE:

NUMBER OF SERVINGS: RECIPE TYPE:

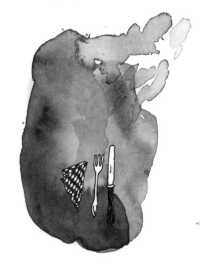

RECIPE FOR:

GIVEN TO ME BY:

DATE:

NUMBER OF SERVINGS: RECIPE TYPE:

RECIPE FOR: _____

GIVEN TO ME BY: _____

DATE: _____

NUMBER OF SERVINGS: _____ RECIPE TYPE: _____

_____
_____
_____
_____
_____
_____
_____
_____
_____
_____
_____
_____
_____
_____
_____
_____
_____
_____
_____
_____
_____
_____
_____
_____
_____

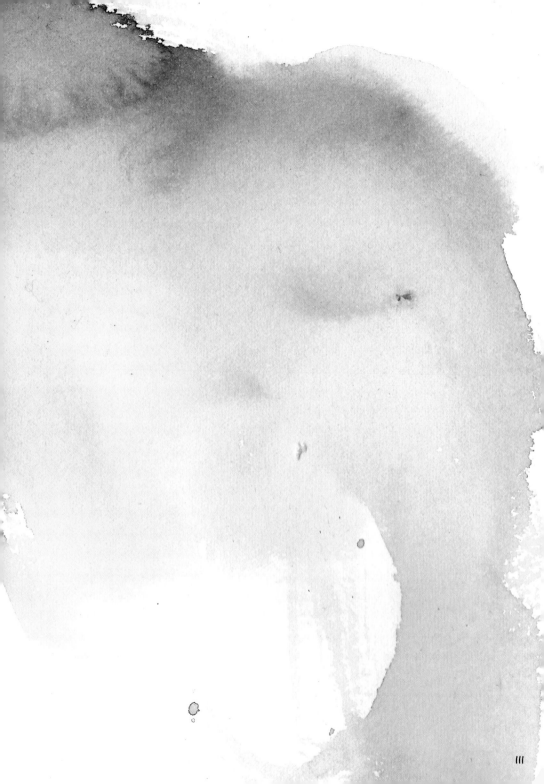

RECIPE FOR:

GIVEN TO ME BY:

DATE:

NUMBER OF SERVINGS: RECIPE TYPE:

RECIPE FOR:

GIVEN TO ME BY:

DATE:

NUMBER OF SERVINGS: RECIPE TYPE:

RECIPE FOR:

GIVEN TO ME BY:

DATE:

NUMBER OF SERVINGS: RECIPE TYPE:

RECIPE FOR:

GIVEN TO ME BY:

DATE:

NUMBER OF SERVINGS: RECIPE TYPE:

RECIPE FOR:

GIVEN TO ME BY:

DATE:

NUMBER OF SERVINGS: RECIPE TYPE:

RECIPE FOR:

GIVEN TO ME BY:

DATE:

NUMBER OF SERVINGS: RECIPE TYPE:

RECIPE FOR:

GIVEN TO ME BY:

DATE:

NUMBER OF SERVINGS: RECIPE TYPE:

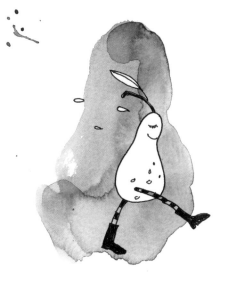

RECIPE FOR: _____

GIVEN TO ME BY: _____

DATE: _____

NUMBER OF SERVINGS: _____ RECIPE TYPE: _____

_____

_____

_____

_____

_____

_____

_____

_____

_____

_____

_____

_____

_____

_____

_____

_____

_____

_____

_____

_____

_____

_____

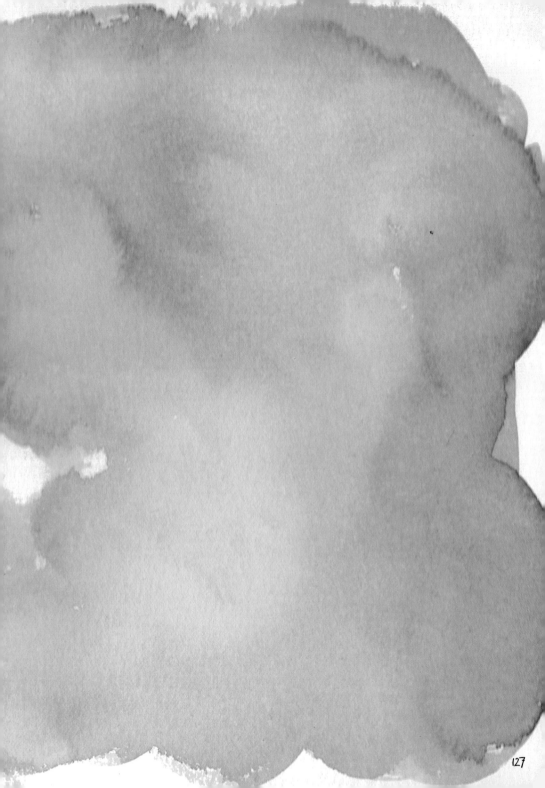

RECIPE FOR:

GIVEN TO ME BY:

DATE:

NUMBER OF SERVINGS: RECIPE TYPE:

RECIPE FOR:

GIVEN TO ME BY:

DATE:

NUMBER OF SERVINGS: RECIPE TYPE:

RECIPE FOR:

GIVEN TO ME BY:

DATE:

NUMBER OF SERVINGS: RECIPE TYPE:

RECIPE FOR:

GIVEN TO ME BY:

DATE:

NUMBER OF SERVINGS: RECIPE TYPE:

RECIPE FOR:

GIVEN TO ME BY:

DATE:

NUMBER OF SERVINGS: RECIPE TYPE:

RECIPE FOR: _____

GIVEN TO ME BY: _____

DATE: _____

NUMBER OF SERVINGS: _____ RECIPE TYPE: _____

_____

_____

_____

_____

_____

_____

_____

_____

_____

_____

_____

_____

_____

_____

_____

_____

_____

_____

_____

_____

_____

_____

_____

_____

_____

_____

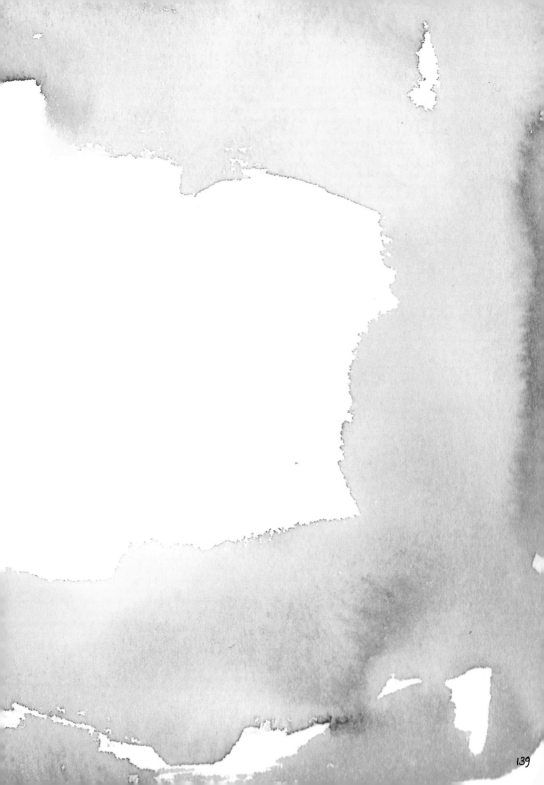

RECIPE FOR:

GIVEN TO ME BY:

DATE:

NUMBER OF SERVINGS: RECIPE TYPE:

FEED
ME

RECIPE FOR:

GIVEN TO ME BY:

DATE:

NUMBER OF SERVINGS: RECIPE TYPE:

RECIPE FOR: _____

GIVEN TO ME BY: _____

DATE: _____

NUMBER OF SERVINGS: _____   RECIPE TYPE: _____

_____

_____

_____

_____

_____

_____

_____

_____

_____

_____

_____

_____

_____

_____

_____

_____

_____

_____

_____

_____

_____

RECIPE FOR:

GIVEN TO ME BY:

DATE:

NUMBER OF SERVINGS: RECIPE TYPE:

RECIPE FOR:

GIVEN TO ME BY:

DATE:

NUMBER OF SERVINGS: RECIPE TYPE:

RECIPE FOR:

GIVEN TO ME BY:

DATE:

NUMBER OF SERVINGS: RECIPE TYPE:

RECIPE FOR: _____

GIVEN TO ME BY: _____

DATE: _____

NUMBER OF SERVINGS: _____   RECIPE TYPE: _____

iNDEX

PAGE

B

C

D

E

F

G

H

i

j

k

L

PAGE

M

N

O

157

P

PAGE

Q

R

S

U

V

W

XYZ   PAGE

SO LONG
BITCHES!